Dinosaur - The Plays

Two plays for reading in groups

Written by

Ian MacDonald

Illustrated by Derry Dillon

First published
January 05 in Great Britain by

Educational Printing Services Limited
Albion Mill, Water Street, Great Harwood, Blackburn BB6 7QR
Telephone: (01254) 882080   Fax: (01254) 882010
E-mail: enquiries@eprint.co.uk   Website: www.eprint.co.uk

ISBN 1-904904-15-7

Mrs Wrelton's Dinosaur

and

Spike's Tail

Two plays adapted from the original stories by the same author.

How to use this book:

Here are two plays which are great fun to read in a small group. Share the parts out: main characters will need a reader each, while others can take on two minor characters quite easily. The part of Spike may be read by the same person who plays Sam; you will see why as you begin to read the first play.

If, later, you decide to perform this to your friends, or another class in school, you do not need any special props; a table and a few chairs can represent a classroom or a train carriage. Alternatively, it is great fun to record the plays on tape. You can really use your imagination to create the sound effects such as the school playground or the train station.

Have fun!

Contents

Mrs Wrelton's Dinosaur

Characters:

Main Characters:

Sam	Suhail
Amy	Mrs Wrelton
Narrator	Spike

Minor Characters:

Ben	Sam's Mum
Mrs Shawcross	Amy's Doll
Mrs Bansel	Mrs Johnson

Sound effects: A cat, a bumping noise and a ray-gun

Scene 1: In the Classroom

(The Scene is a classroom for younger children with a carpet area, a sand tray and play bricks scattered on a table. In the book corner stands a big green dinosaur.)

Narrator:	Here is Mrs Wrelton's class. They are all seated on the carpet while she calls the register.
Mrs Wrelton:	Sam?

Sam:	Yes, Mrs Wrelton.
Mrs Wrelton:	Suhail?
Suhail:	Yes, Mrs Wrelton.
Mrs Wrelton:	Amy?
Amy:	Yes, Mrs Wrelton.
Mrs Wrelton:	Spike?
Narrator:	There was no answer. So Mrs Wrelton tried again.
Mrs Wrelton:	Spike?
Spike:	Yes, Mrs Wrelton.
Narrator:	Spike was the name of the

big green dinosaur. He was
Sam's best friend in all the
world.

Mrs Wrelton: Now, we have a new boy
here today. His name is Ben.
I want you all to be nice to
him and show him where
everything is.

Ben: Who's Spike?

Sam: Come on I'll show you.

(Sam, Amy and Suhail wander off to the book corner.)

Sam: Here he is. This is Spike.

Ben: Wow! He's great. He's got

spikes all sticking up along his back. And just look at his long green tail! I can't tell if he's grinning or growling.

Sam: I think it's a grinning day. You never can tell with Spike. He can't move his mouth.

Ben: Is that why you answered the register for him?

Sam: Yes, that's right.

Ben: What is he? Is he a Tyrannosaurus Rex?

Amy: I think he's a Brontosaurus.

Suhail:	No, he's definitely a Stegosaurus. Look at his long green tail with the triangle spikes all sticking up.
Sam:	Suhail knows everything about dinosaurs.
Amy:	He's made of paper and glue.
Suhail:	It's called papier-mâché.
Sam:	He was made a long time ago by Mrs Wrelton's old class.
Suhail:	Maybe long ago like when there were dinosaurs.

Narrator:	Just then Mrs Shawcross, the Headteacher, came into the classroom.
Mrs Wrelton:	Now children, Mrs Shawcross has got something exciting to tell us. All come and sit here on the carpet and listen.
Mrs Shawcross:	Do you remember children, that you are going to have a new classroom?
Children:	Yes, Mrs Shawcross.
Mrs Shawcross:	And after the holiday you will be able to move into it. There will be a new play corner, new shelves for the

books and a new sink too. It will be lovely.

Sam: *(In a whisper)* Do you remember when they knocked down the old classrooms?

Amy: Yes, it was great. There were diggers and big machines everywhere.

Suhail: And then we were allowed to watch when the builders made a new school with a tiled roof.

Ben: Wow! That must have been great!

Mrs Wrelton: Be quiet children. Mrs Shawcross is talking.

Mrs Shawcross: Now children, this will be a good opportunity to have a big tidy up. Tomorrow, on the playground, there will be a big yellow skip. It's for putting all the rubbish in. I want you to stay away from it. We don't want anyone falling in and getting hurt.

Amy: Perhaps Mrs Wrelton will put in the computer that does not work.

Suhail: It doesn't work because Ryan put his sandwich where the disk should go.

Mrs Wrelton: Will you stop talking!

Mrs Shawcross: Now you must all help Mrs Wrelton to tidy the classroom and throw away all the things that we don't want in the new school *(as she says this she looks across at Spike.)*

Scene 2: In the Classroom Again

(The classroom is arranged as usual but there is now a big yellow skip outside the window.)

Narrator: That night Sam did not sleep very well. He was worried about Spike. When he got to school the next day he rushed in and was pleased to see that Spike was in his usual place.

| Suhail: | Come and look. The skip is on the playground! |

(They all rush outside to see.)

| Sam: | Wow, just look at all the things in there. |

| Amy: | I'm going to climb up and have a look. |

| Suhail: | But Mrs Shawcross said we weren't to go near the skip. She said it was dangerous. |

(Amy climbs up anyway.)

| Amy: | There's some of our old classroom toys in here. I can see a jigsaw, some old |

chairs and a teddy with his arm missing.

Suhail:	Look out, here comes Mrs Shawcross!
Sam:	Let's go back inside. At least Spike is still there.
Mrs Wrelton:	Now, everyone on the carpet for the register. Sam?
Sam:	Yes, Mrs Wrelton.
Mrs Wrelton:	Suhail?
Suhail:	Yes, Mrs Wrelton.
Mrs Wrelton:	Amy?

Amy:	Yes, Mrs Wrelton.
Mrs Wrelton:	Spike?
Spike:	Yes, Mrs Wrelton.
Mrs Wrelton:	Now I want you to start to have a tidy up. Some of you can do those trays over there. And Suhail and Sam, you can sharpen the pencils. Throw away any that are too small to use.

(Sam and Suhail go over to the pencil trays.)

Suhail:	Sam, will you sit next to me in the new classroom?
Sam:	Of course I will. But as long

as Amy can sit on our table too. And we have to be near Spike.

Suhail: That's alright. I want to be near Spike as well.

Narrator: But later, after the children had been out to play, they came back... and Spike was gone.

Mrs Wrelton: Now children. I've a lovely story to read to you. Sit here on the carpet.

Sam: *(Whispering)* Do you know what's happened to Spike?

Suhail: No. Where's he gone?

Ben:	Ha, ha, I thought you were supposed to know everything about dinosaurs.
Amy:	Oh, be quiet, Ben!
Sam:	Look, outside the window. There's Spike. He's in the skip!
Amy:	So he is. I can see his green spikes all sticking up!
Sam:	We've got to do something.
Mrs Wrelton:	Sam, will you stop talking while I'm trying to read a story!
Sam:	(Whispering) We've got to do something.

Suhail:	What can we do?
Amy:	We're not allowed near the skip anyway. I nearly got into trouble before.
Sam:	Well, I'm going to do something even if you're not.
Sam:	*(Going over to the window and whispering to Spike.)* Don't worry, Spike. It's going to be alright. I'm going to rescue you.

Scene 3:   Around the Houses

(Sam and his mum and dad are eating their dinner.)

Narrator: Back at home Sam could not
                  stop thinking about Spike.
                  He had a plan.

Mum: Is something the matter,
                  Sam?

Sam: No. I'm fine.

Mum:	But you've hardly touched your dinner.
Sam:	I'm just not very hungry.
Mum:	But it's your favourite, burgers and beans. There won't be anything else.
Sam:	Mum. Can I go round to Suhail's house?
Mum:	Have you asked his mum?
Sam:	Yes. She said it would be O.K.
Mum:	Alright then. Just for an hour, mind. You've got the whole holiday to see Suhail, you know.

Narrator:	Sam went to the front door. On the way he collected his coat, a baseball cap and his dad's golf club... just in case there were monsters! Soon he arrived at Suhail's house.
Suhail:	*(Opening the door)* Hello, Sam. What are you doing here?
Sam:	I'm going to rescue Spike. Are you coming?
Mrs Bansel:	*(From inside the house)* Who is it, Suhail?
Sam:	Can you come out or not?
Suhail:	But I have to tidy my room.

Sam:	Ask if you can come to my house, then.
Suhail:	*(Calling to his mum)* Mum, can I go to Sam's house?
Mrs Bansel:	*(From inside)* Alright, Suhail. But make sure you are back in an hour.
Sam:	It might be dangerous. Can you bring something useful with you?
Suhail:	Wait here. *(Suhail goes indoors and comes back wearing a superhero mask and carrying a plastic ray-gun.)* Look at this ray-gun. It lights up when you fire it.

Sam:	Come on let's go.
Suhail:	Let's try Amy too.
Narrator:	Soon Sam and Suhail were at Amy's house. They rang the bell and Amy opened the door.
Amy:	What are you doing here?
Sam:	We're going to rescue Spike. Are you coming to help us?
Suhail:	You've got to bring something with you for the adventure.
Amy:	Wait here.

Narrator:	Amy went away and came back carrying a doll. She pulled a cord and the doll spoke.
Doll:	I am wearing my lovely blue dress.
Suhail:	*(Whispering to Suhail)* I don't know what good that will be.
Sam:	Never mind. We must hurry - there might not be much time.

Scene 4: Back at School

Narrator:	Soon Sam, Suhail and Amy were back at the school gate. It was already beginning to get dark.
Sam:	Get down low. There might be people about. We don't want anyone to see us!

Suhail:	Look. There's Mr Griffin, the caretaker, carrying his keys. Soon he'll be locking up the gates.
Amy:	Look out, there's a lorry coming. I can see its headlights.
Suhail:	Let's wait until it has gone by. Then it will be safe to go.
Amy:	There! It's gone in now. Look, it will be alright now.
Sam:	When I say now, we'll go as far as the shed on the playground. NOW!

Amy: Quick, let's hide there where it's nice and dark. There's a shadow just behind the shed.

Sam: If we go around the edge of the small playground there is less chance of anyone coming by.

Suhail: Good idea. If there are any teachers they will go across the big playground.

Amy: And there will be bushes to hide in too.

Sam: Come on. Let's hurry.

(Sam, Suhail and Amy climb into the bushes at the edge and begin to make their way slowly along the edge of the playground.)

Amy: Great! It's even darker in here!

Suhail: Well, I don't like it. It's hard work walking through here. The bushes are all prickly. Can't we go on the playground now?

Amy: No we can't, Suhail. Someone might see us.

Sam: Don't worry, I've got my dad's golf club with me. I will bash the bushes down so we can go along.

Amy:	Won't he be cross if you get his club all scratched?
Sam:	I think he will understand that it is important to rescue Spike.
Amy:	My dad would go mad if I took his things and ruined them.
Suhail:	Aaargh! Look, there's a snake.
Sam:	Stand back. I will give it a bash with my club.
Amy:	Don't be silly! Look, it's just an old piece of rope.

Narrator:	The children went a bit further hardly daring to speak in case anything else appeared in their way.
Suhail:	Stop! Listen! Can you hear something?
Sam:	I can't hear anything.
Suhail:	I can. I think there's something coming this way.
Amy:	Ooh, and now it's gone all light... I can hardly see!
Sam:	Look there's a giant cat on the playground. There's its shadow.

(The sound of a cat meowing is heard.)

Suhail: Run!

Doll: My hair needs brushing.

Sam: Can't you stop your doll making that noise.

Doll: Can I wear my red dress?

Suhail: Turn it off! The giant cat will hear and come and get us.

Amy: Stop worrying. Look, it's just the school cat up there on the roof.

Suhail: Oh, so it is. It's standing in front of the light.

Sam:	That's why its shadow is so big.
Sam:	Come on before anything else happens.
Narrator:	Sam, Suhail and Amy went on past the classrooms, past the office where Mrs Southall did the letters and were soon at the place where the children hung their coats.
Sam:	Come on, it's not far now. Keep together. It can't be far.
Suhail:	But what if someone sees us?

Sam:	We'll just have to take a chance. We can't go back now.
Doll:	Can I go for a walk?
Sam:	Amy!
Suhail:	Amy!
Amy:	Sorry!
Suhail:	Take the batteries out and then it can't say anything else.
Amy:	Alright... but I don't know what you're so scared of.
Suhail:	I'm not scared. I just don't

like what your doll says,
that's all.

Sam: Be quiet both of you. Stop
arguing. We've got to rescue
Spike, remember?

*(The three children stop in their tracks as
they hear a new noise: Thump! Thump! Bump!)*

Sam: What is it?

Amy: It's big and green... and look
at its great gaping mouth.

Suhail: It's a big green alien and it's
coming to get us! *(There is
the sound of Suhail's
ray-gun: Whoo-whoo.)*

Sam:	Aaaah!
Amy:	Help!
Suhail:	Mummy!

(Suhail and Amy turn to run but Sam stops them.)

Sam:	Stop! It's only the green litter bin.
Suhail:	What! It can't be. What about its big mouth?
Amy:	Sam's right, look. That's the hole where we put our rubbish.
Suhail:	Something's coming out. Be careful!

Sam: Look, it's only a little squirrel. He's got someone's left over apple for his dinner.

Amy: Come on, let's hurry up and find Spike. I want to go home.

Sam: The skip is just around the next corner.

Narrator: The children crept along the wall and around the next corner and they all looked at the place where the skip had been.

Suhail: Where is it? I thought you said the skip was here.

Amy: Where's Spike?

Sam: He's gone!

Scene 5: Back Home

Narrator: Sam, Suhail and Amy went
back home. When they got
there three mums were
waiting. They were all very
cross.

Mum: Where have you been?

Mrs Bansel: We've been very worried.

Mrs Johnson:	And just look at the mess you're in!
Amy:	But we only went to school.
Suhail:	It was Sam's idea.
Sam:	But we had to rescue Spike!
Mum:	No playing out again for you... not for a whole week.
Mrs Bansel:	And that goes for you too, young man.
Mrs Johnson:	And you, my girl!
Narrator:	The next week was the school holidays. Sam was not allowed out to see his friends. But he did not care.

He just missed Spike. His mum came into his room.

Mum: What's the matter, Sam?

Sam: Nothing.

Mum: I know I was cross with you about going to school the other day, but I was worried that you might have got lost or something.

Sam: It's alright.

Mum: But you haven't come out of your room for three days now. And look at all these dinosaur pictures. I can hardly see the wallpaper!

Sam: They're all pictures of Spike. I miss him, Mum. He was in the skip and I went to rescue him but the skip had gone and it was all my fault.

Mum: But it wasn't your fault. You did your best... even if it was silly to go back to school in the dark.

Sam: I won't ever see Spike again, though, will I?

Mum: Never mind. Soon it will be time to go back to school and see the nice new classrooms. That will be exciting, won't it?

Sam: But it won't be the same. Not without Spike there.

Mum: Now, I think you are tired. Put your pencils away and try to go to sleep. Perhaps you will feel better in the morning.

Scene 6: In the New Classroom

(As children arrive at the school gate they are excited to see the new classroom.)

Narrator: The next day Sam got out of bed and dressed for school. He usually called for Suhail and Amy on the way but this morning he felt like walking on his own. They both met him in the playground.

Suhail:	Sam! Sam! Look at the new classroom. It's been built while we have been away on holiday.
Amy:	I can see through the window. There's new shelves and new coat pegs and everything.
Suhail:	Sam, will you sit next to me in the new classroom? You said you would.
Sam:	*(Grumpily)* I suppose so. It doesn't matter really. It won't be the same... not without Spike.
Amy:	Cheer up Sam. It will be fun

	to see all the new things inside.
Sam:	I don't want to see the new classroom. I want the old classroom back where Spike was.
Mrs Wrelton:	Hello Sam. It's nearly time for the bell to go. Can you come in and help me tidy some things in the book corner?
Sam:	Alright.
Narrator:	Sam went into the new classroom. He looked about him. He looked at the new pegs, the new pictures on

the wall and the new books on the shelves.

Mrs Wrelton: Look here, Sam. Here is the place where you will sit.

Sam: It doesn't matter where I sit.

Mrs Wrelton: But your friend is sitting there already.

Sam: SPIKE!

Mrs Wrelton: I just couldn't throw him away after all.

Suhail: *(Rushing in)* Look, Spike's here!

Amy:	Mrs Wrelton rescued him from the skip!
Sam:	So is he going to be here in the new classroom with us?
Mrs Wrelton:	No, not really, Sam. He is too big to be in this classroom.
Amy:	But he can sit here with us like he always used to.
Suhail:	He can sit by the book corner and watch us do our work.
Mrs Wrelton:	I'm afraid there isn't room. We've got lots of new things and there isn't really room for a big green dinosaur.

Sam:	But you're not going to throw him away again are you?
Mrs Wrelton:	No, of course not. But we need to find a good home for him. I don't think he will like it here in the new classroom.
Amy:	But where can he live?
Suhail:	You can't put a dinosaur just anywhere. He's got to be looked after.
Mrs Wrelton:	No we can't. Do you know anyone who could look after him properly?

Sam: I could.

Mrs Wrelton: Could you?

Scene 7: In Sam's Bedroom

(It is night-time in Sam's room and two shapes can be seen under the covers.)

Narrator: It was dark and Mum put her head around the door to say goodnight to Sam.

Mum: Sam, are you asleep?

Sam: I'm nearly asleep.

Mum: Have you got enough room in there?

Sam: Yes, Mum. I'm quite comfy!

Mum: Goodnight then, Sam.

Sam: Goodnight, Mum. Goodnight, Spike.

Spike: Goodnight, Sam.

Spike's Tail

Characters:

Main Characters:

Sam	Mum
Suhail	Spike
Narrator	

Minor Characters:

Ticket Man (at the station)

Old Lady

Museum Man (Palaeontologist)

Ticket Lady (at the museum)

Four Voices

Sound effects:

Underground train doors,

A tyrannosaurus roaring.

Scene 1: In Sam's Bedroom

(Sam is in bed. It is dark and the curtains are gently moving.)

Narrator: It was dark in Sam's bedroom. The curtains gently moved at the window. Strange shadows formed on the carpet. Sam felt as if he could hear strange voices inside his head.

Sam: It must be the middle of the night. What's that scratching noise?

Voice 1: Sam, watch out, there's someone at the window.

Voice 2: Sam, beware, there's someone at the door.

Voice 3: Sam, watch out, pull the covers tight about your ears.

Voice 4: Sam, beware, there's a monster at the door.

Sam:	*(Whispers to himself)* It's a good job there's a dinosaur in my bed!
Mum:	Sam! Are you up yet?
Sam:	Yawn!
Mum:	Sam, I'm coming in. *(Slowly the door opens.)*
Sam:	Aaargh! It's Monster Mum!
Spike:	Oh no, not Monster Mum!
Mum:	Good morning, Sam.
Sam:	Good morning, Mum.
Mum:	Good morning, Spike.

Spike:	Good morning, Monster Mum.
Mum:	Don't be cheeky! Now come on both of you, it's time to get up.
Sam:	Do we have to? It's nice and warm in here. Besides, Spike's not woken up properly yet.
Mum:	Yes, you do have to get up. Have you forgotten what today is?
Sam:	What is it?
Mum:	Today we are off to the dinosaur museum, remember?

Sam:	Great!
Spike:	Yippee!
Mum:	Come on then. Had you forgotten? I said you could bring a friend. Who is it going to be?
Sam:	Brilliant! I can choose one of my friends.
Spike:	What about Amy?
Sam:	She can kick a football all the way to the end of the playground. She can make her face like an alien.
Mum:	*(Raising her eyebrows)* Well, that's really useful!

Spike: What about Suhail?

Sam: Suhail knows everything about dinosaurs... and we are going to a dinosaur museum.

Mum: Well, it's up to you. You'll have to ring him now or they might have gone out.

Sam: It's Suhail. He will know the names of all the dinosaurs.

Mum: Hurry up then and ring Suhail.

Sam: Come on, Spike. We've got to get up. We're going to the dinosaur museum.

Spike: What's a museum?

Scene 2: To the Train Station

Narrator: So Sam phoned Suhail and found out that he was allowed to come. Soon Sam was dressed and having his breakfast. Just then the doorbell rang.

Mum: That must be Suhail. Hurry up and get your coat.

Sam:	Can I wear my baseball cap?
Mum:	Of course you can. Now go and open the front door.

(Sam opens the door to Suhail.)

Suhail:	Hi, Sam. Isn't it exciting! Are we really going to see dinosaurs?
Sam:	Yes! It's going to be great. Spike will love it too.
Mum:	Hello, Suhail. That's a smart new coat. Is it new?
Suhail:	Yes, my mum bought it for me yesterday.
Mum:	Come on, Sam or we'll be late. You haven't even got your coat on yet.

Sam:	I've just got to get Spike. I won't be a minute.
Mum:	What did you say, Sam?
Sam:	I said I'm just going to get Spike.
Mum:	Spike? I'm afraid Spike can't come.
Sam:	But we're going to see dinosaurs. We can't leave Spike behind.
Mum:	But he's just too big to take on the train.
Sam:	But I can carry him. I wouldn't mind.
Mum:	I'm sorry, love, but it will be

far too busy in London for a
big green dinosaur.

Sam: But he could come instead
of Suhail.

Suhail: Boo hoo!

Mum: Oh, Sam!

Sam: I didn't mean that I didn't
want Suhail to come... it's
just that I can't leave Spike
behind.

Mum: It's no good, Sam. You'll
have to forget the idea.

Suhail: But I want to go to the
museum and see the
dinosaurs.

Mum:	Of course you are coming to the museum, Suhail. Now come on both of you or we'll be late.
Narrator:	Soon Sam, Mum and Suhail had gone out of the house and down the road, past the newspaper shop and were headed for the station.
Sam:	Please Mum!
Mum:	No, Sam!
Suhail:	Are we nearly at the station?
Sam:	Please Mum. He wouldn't be any trouble.
Mum:	Just stop it, Sam.

Suhail:	Ooh! Look, there's the station.
Sam:	Please, I'll carry him everywhere, and I won't complain, and Spike will be really good.
Mum:	Sam!
Suhail:	I can see a train.

72

Scene 3: At the Station

(They arrive at the station and go to a little window where a man in a peaked cap is selling train tickets.)

Narrator: Eventually they were at the station. They went to the window to buy a ticket. First there was Mum, then there was Suhail. Then there was Sam... and then there was Spike!

Sam:	Thanks, Mum.
Suhail:	Doesn't Spike look smart in your baseball cap, Sam?
Mum:	*(Sighs)* Just remember, he's your responsibility.
Spike:	I'm a sponsy-bility!
Mum:	*(To the ticket man)* Can I have one adult and two children to London, please.
Sam:	And Spike.
Suhail:	*(Whispering)* Dinosaurs don't need tickets on trains, Sam.
Ticket Man:	Let me see now. Here are your tickets, one adult and

two boys. You sure that's all?

Mum: Yes! What do you mean?

Ticket Man: What about your dragon there?

Mum: What dragon?

Sam: He's not a dragon. He's a dinosaur.

Suhail: He's a Stegosaurus.

Ticket Man: Oh, I see. Wait a minute; I'll have to have a look in my book.

Mum: Oh, do please hurry up. We don't want to miss our train.

Ticket Man:	Let's see ... cats ... dogs ... parrots. No, I can't see anything here about dinosaurs.
Suhail:	Does that mean he can't go on the train?
Sam:	Please! Please!
Ticket man:	*(Winking)* I suppose we'll just have to let him go free then, won't we.
Mum:	Thank goodness for that. Now, let's hurry up, boys. Look, the train is just coming.
Suhail:	But you've got to have a ticket. A ticket man will

want to see it when we get
to London.

Sam: There's a ticket. Look, there
on the platform *(he picks it
up)*.

Suhail: Someone's made a hole in it.

Sam: I'm going to give it to Spike.
Here, I'll put it in the front
of Spike's cap.

Suhail: Spike looks pleased.

Mum: The train's here now. Come
on, climb up. Watch the
step.

Sam: Up you go, Spike. Be careful.

Spike: I be careful.

Suhail: He only just fits through the door. They didn't think of dinosaurs when they made trains did they?

Mum: Let's sit down here. Do you boys want to sit by the window?

Sam: Spike might want to see out. He might want to be by the window.

Suhail: Dinosaurs are not used to going on trains. He might find it a bit scary.

Sam: You know everything about dinosaurs, Suhail.

Suhail:	I know. Shall I sit here by the window instead?
Sam:	O.K.
Mum:	We're off. Thank goodness!
Narrator:	The train pulled away from the station. The houses were soon left behind and they were out in the countryside.
Suhail:	Look, look. I can see trees and fields.
Sam:	And cows and sheep.
Mum:	And, there, can you see a farmer on his tractor?

Sam:	But soon, we're going to see dinosaurs.
Narrator:	The train went through lots of stations. At one station a lady got on to the train. She was wearing a purple hat with a big feather in it.
Mum:	Can I help you with your bag? It looks very heavy.
Old Lady:	*(Puffing)* Thank you very much. That's very kind of you.
Suhail:	*(Whispering)* Look at that big feather in her hat, Sam.
Sam:	*(Whispering also)* I know. It's enormous!

Mum:	There's a spare seat here. Would you like me to put your bag up on the rack?
Old Lady:	Thank you. Goodness me!
Mum:	Oh dear, you've dropped your hat. Let me pick it up for you.
Old Lady:	What on earth is that big green thing?
Sam:	Don't worry. It's only Spike.
Old Lady:	A spike?
Suhail:	No, not a spike. Just Spike. He belongs to Sam.

Old Lady:	What on earth is it doing on the train? Will it bite?
Mum:	Don't worry he can't hurt you. He's only made of paper and glue.
Suhail:	He's a Stegosaurus.
Old Lady:	A what?
Sam:	It's a kind of dinosaur.
Suhail:	We're going to see some more dinosaurs, in London.
Old Lady:	There are more of these monsters in London. Oh, dear!

Mum: Do sit down. I think the train is about to go.

Old Lady: I don't think I shall sit here after all. No, I think I will go on to the next carriage, if you don't mind. *(She hurries away.)*

Sam: What was the matter with her?

Suhail: I think she was afraid of Spike.

Mum: Sit down, boys. One more station and we're in London.

Suhail: Hurray!

Sam: Hurray!

Spike: Hoo-ray!

Scene 4: On the Underground

(Sam, Suhail, Mum and Spike are walking through the Underground tunnels. There are lots of other travellers hurrying to catch their trains.)

Narrator: Soon they had arrived in London. Mum said that they had to go on the underground train to get to the dinosaur museum. To get to the underground trains they had to go on a moving staircase.

Suhail:	Wow, look, the stairs are moving. The stairs do the walking for you.
Mum:	Hold onto Spike tightly. We don't want any accidents.
Sam:	What's this called, Mum?
Mum:	The moving stairs? It's called an escalator.
Spike:	Ess-key-later.
Sam:	Well done, Spike. You've learned a new word.
Suhail:	Dinosaurs don't know about escalators. They didn't have them in dinosaur times.

Sam:	But what if you had to go up a mountain, or something?
Suhail:	Then you just had to walk.
Mum:	Here we are... and there's the underground train already in the platform.
Suhail:	Just look at all the people in the train!
Mum:	Mind the sliding doors, Sam.

(There is a sound of hissing as the doors close.)

Sam:	Are we nearly there, yet?
Mum:	We've only just got on this train.

Suhail:	It's all dark outside. There isn't any sunshine down here.
Mum:	We have to go a few stops on the underground. Look up there, above your head. You can see the names of the stations there.
Sam:	King's Cross.
Suhail:	Covent Garden.
Sam:	Green Park.
Suhail:	Piccadilly Circus.
Sam:	Will there be clowns at Piccadilly Circus?

Mum:	No, Sam. Those are just the names of the stations.
Spike:	No clowns?
Suhail:	Never mind, Spike. We're going to see the dinosaurs soon.
Mum:	Come on, we're here. Time to get off!
Suhail:	It says Kensington on the sign. Is this where the dinosaur museum is?
Mum:	Yes, this is our stop.
Sam/Suhail:	Hurray!

Spike:	Hoo-ray! Hoo-ray! Hoo-ray!
Mum:	Come on, off we get.
Suhail:	We're here! We're here!
Sam:	Come on Spike off we get, onto the platform.
Mum:	Mind the step, Suhail.
Sam:	Oh wait, Mum. My shoelace has come undone *(he bends down to tie his shoelace).*
Mum:	Don't stop, there, Sam. It's not safe to stop by the edge of the platform.
Sam:	I won't be a minute.

Suhail: Look out. The sliding doors are shutting! *(The sound of doors closing is heard: PSSHH!... BIFF!... CRUMP!)* Look, Sam. Spike's jumped. He must be really excited.

Sam: But he's never done a jump before!

Mum: Come on, Sam. The train is moving. Come away.

Suhail: Look! Look! Spike's tail has gone! The train has eaten Spike's tail.

Sam: Mum! The train has eaten Spike's tail.

Suhail:	Spike's tail is still on the train... it's going off to Piccadilly Circus.
Sam:	Suhail, why didn't you tell me that train's ate dinosaur tails?
Mum:	Don't be silly, Sam. How was he supposed to know that? Suhail doesn't know everything.
Sam:	But he knows everything about dinosaurs. Why didn't he tell me that the train was going to bite Spike's tail off?
Suhail:	Boo hoo!

Mum:	Never mind, Sam. be alright. When we the museum it will tak mind off it. Here's a tissue to dry your eyes.
Suhail:	*(Even louder)* Boo hoo!
Mum:	And you, Suhail. Dry your eyes now. Cheer up, we're going to the museum now.
Narrator:	They left the station platform and went to the next escalator to take them up to the dinosaur museum.
Mum:	Come on, boys. Climb on to the escalator. Be careful now.

ail:	Why are the people running on the escalator? You don't have to walk on it. It's moving anyway.
Mum:	They're just in a hurry... and so are we!
Sam:	Mum, the people are bumping Spike.
Mum:	Just hold on tight to him.

(Someone bumps into Sam and he lets go of Spike.)

Suhail:	Sam! You've dropped Spike. He's falling down the escalator.

Sam:	Mum! Mum! Spike has gone down the upstairs!
Mum:	Stay there, Sam. Don't do anything silly!
Sam:	I'm coming Spike. Don't worry, I'm coming.
Suhail:	Sam! I'm up here. Where are you going?
Sam:	I'm going to get Spike. He doesn't know where to go. I can't leave him there at the bottom. He might be scared.
Mum:	Sam, wait there. Where are you going?

Suhail:	Look, Sam's going down the down escalator.
Mum:	Oh, Sam!
Suhail:	And now Spike's coming up the up escalator on his own.
Sam:	Mum! Mum! Spike's been clever. He has found a lady to bring him up the upstairs.
Suhail:	Sam, Spike's here now. Come back up.
Mum:	Let's go to the museum before anything else happens.

Scene 5: At the Museum

(Inside the museum people are queuing to buy tickets.)

Narrator: Sam, Suhail, Mum and Spike
arrived at the museum and
went inside. Mum queued up
to buy tickets.

Ticket Lady:	Hello, can I help you?
Mum:	Yes, please. I'd like three tickets please. One adult and two children.
Ticket Lady:	There we are. And would you like to buy a guide book?
Mum:	No, thank you.
Sam:	Suhail knows everything about dinosaurs so we don't need to buy a guidebook.
Ticket Lady:	And do you want to leave your luggage in the cloakroom.
Mum:	No, we can carry our coats, thank you.

Ticket Lady:	I meant that thing.
Sam:	That's not luggage. That's Spike.
Suhail:	He's a stegosaurus.
Ticket lady:	Well, suit yourself. The dinosaur gallery is that way. Enjoy your visit.
Mum:	Well, she wasn't very nice, was she?
Sam:	Anyway, at least we didn't have to buy a ticket for Spike.
Suhail:	You don't have to buy a ticket for a dinosaur in a dinosaur museum.

Mum:	Look, Sam, at how beautiful this room is. It's full of plants and flowers.
Suhail:	Wow! Just look at how big the rooms are here. Come on, Sam. Come and look at everything!
Sam:	I don't feel like it.
Suhail:	Why not?
Sam:	I'm worried about Spike. He just doesn't look right without his tail.
Mum:	Well, we've paid a lot of money to get in. You'll just have to forget about Spike

	for now and try and enjoy yourself.
Suhail:	Wow! Look in here. A whole room full of wild animals.
Sam:	Huh! They're not real anyway. They're not moving or making a noise.
Mum:	Oh, do try and cheer up, Sam.
Suhail:	Look. There are tigers and bears and lions... and everything.
Sam:	And they've all got tails... and Spike hasn't.
Mum:	Oh, Sam!

Narrator:	Just then Suhail spotted an enormous skeleton of a whale in the next room. He ran to stand inside it.
Suhail:	Look! Look! I'm inside the whale. It's nearly as big as a brontosaurus... and it's eaten me all up. Come on Sam.
Sam:	No thanks. Spike's been nearly eaten once already today. I'm not taking any chances.
Mum:	Oh, Sam. Now it's nearly one-o-clock. I think it's time we all had some lunch.
Narrator:	They all went into the restaurant and found a

table. Mum bought burgers
and chips for everybody.

Suhail: Great! Burgers and chips.
My favourite!

Mum: Come on Sam. You like
burgers and chips. Don't just
sit there. Your dinner's
getting cold.

Sam: I'm not hungry.

Mum: I've got this especially for
you. Look, there are
pictures of dinosaurs on the
box.

Suhail: Look, that's a Tyrannosaurus
fighting a Stegosaurus.

Sam:	And I bet the Stegosaurus has got a tail... and with spikes sticking up as well.
Suhail:	See the Tyrannosaurus is winning. Look, I'm putting ketchup on the Stegosaurus because he's being eaten up.
Mum:	Don't play with your food, Suhail. And, Sam, you've not eaten anything at all.
Sam:	I'm not hungry, I told you.
Mum:	Well, there won't be anything to eat until we get home. And that will be a long time.

Suhail: Can we go and see the
               dinosaurs now? Can we?
               Can we?

Mum: I think that's a very good
               idea.

Scene 6: In the Dinosaur Room

(In the dinosaur room there are television screens, displays and huge model dinosaurs. Some of the dinosaurs actually move and make a noise.)

Narrator: Suhail ran on ahead into the dinosaur room. Mum followed and Sam trailed behind with Spike.

Suhail: Wow! Look at all the dinosaurs in here. There's a Brontosaurus munching on leaves. And here's a whole family of little ones. Come and look Sam.

Sam: I'm alright. I can see from here.

Mum: Oh, do cheer up Sam. This is what you wanted to do. Please try and enjoy it now we're here.

Suhail. Sam, Sam. Come and see. There's a Stegosaurus just like Spike.

Sam: He's not like Spike. He's got a tail!

Narrator:	Suddenly the Tyrannosaurus turned its head and gave a big roar.
Tyrannosaurus:	ROAR!
Spike:	Roar.
Suhail:	Spike doesn't roar as loudly as the Tyrannosaurus.
Sam:	You don't really feel like roaring properly when not all of you is there.
Mum:	My legs are getting tired, boys. I'm going to have a sit down over here.
Sam:	I'll come and sit too. I don't

want to see anything else anyway.

Narrator: Mum went and sat down on a bench away from the dinosaurs. Sam came too bringing Spike.

Suhail: Sam! Sam! There's a lot more to see. Aren't you coming?

Man: Hello!

(A man is working behind a railing.)

Man: *(Looking at Spike)* What's your name?

Sam: His name is Spike. He's my dinosaur.

Man:	What kind is he?
Suhail:	*(Coming over to see)* He's a Stegosaurus.
Man:	Of course. He's a very fine Stegosaurus too.
Sam:	What are you doing?
Man:	Well, this is the skeleton of a Pterodactyl. It was a flying dinosaur that lived millions of years ago.
Suhail:	Where did you find it?
Man:	We found it in Mexico.
Sam:	Why is it here then?

Suhail:	It looks like a jigsaw puzzle.
Man:	Well, it is a bit. It's my job to put it together, the bits that are here and the bits that aren't.
Sam:	You mean there are bits missing?
Man:	Yes, that's right. When something is this old you are lucky to find a whole skeleton. Usually some of it has been lost and I have to make up the part that is missing.
Mum:	That must be very interesting!

Man: Yes, it is. But it can take a long time. I suppose it is a bit like doing a jigsaw puzzle when someone's lost some of the bits.

Suhail: What's that stuff there?

Man: That's what I use for making the missing bones.

Sam: You're a dinosaur repair man!

Scene 7: Returning Home

(Sam, Suhail, Mum and Spike are on the train returning home.)

Narrator:	On the train going home the lady with the feather in her hat got on the train again.
Old Lady:	Oh dear, oh dear! What a busy day. I'm quite worn out.

Mum:	Here, let me help you with your bag.
Old Lady:	That's very kind of you. Very kind indeed.
Mum:	That's quite alright.
Old Lady:	And the train is so crowded too. Oh dear. I do hope I shall find somewhere to sit.
Mum:	Now why don't you sit there, by the window? There's one seat there.
Old Lady:	Oh yes, so there is. I'll be glad to have a sit down.
Suhail:	(Whispering to Sam) It's

the same lady again, the one
with the purple hat.

Sam: She doesn't seem to
                remember us from this
                morning.

Suhail: And I don't think she's seen
                Spike yet, either.

Mum: Don't point Suhail. It's rude.

Suhail: Just look at the big feather
                in it.

Sam: Where do you think she got
                it from?

Suhail: It looks very old.

Sam:	Perhaps it came from a Pterodactyl.
Spike:	Terry-dack-tile!
Suhail:	Pterodactyls didn't have feathers. At least I don't think so.
Mum:	Boys, will you stop talking about that lady's hat. She'll get cross in a minute... and so will I.
Spike:	You're already cross.
Mum:	Don't be cheeky, Spike.
Suhail:	She's looking over here.

Sam:	Mum, the lady's looking at us. Isn't she being rude?
Mum:	Of course not! Anyway, she's not looking at you at all. She's looking at Spike.
Suhail:	But she saw him before, on the way up.
Mum:	Yes, and she wasn't too sure about him then.
Suhail:	Do you think she's admiring his green, scaly skin.
Sam:	No, I think she likes his triangle spikes sticking up all along his back.

Mum: Or, maybe it's because he's got a red ticket stuck in his baseball cap.

Old Lady: Excuse me. I hope you don't think I'm being rude. But I saw your dinosaur on the train going up.

Sam: That's right. We've just been up to see the dinosaurs in London.

Old Lady: But there's something different about him. Didn't he have a green tail before?

Mum: Yes, that's right.

Sam: But now Spike's got a shiny, new white one!

Talking about the Text

Here are some questions to discuss when you have finished reading this book.

1. What clues are there in the text to tell you that this is a play?

2. What is the purpose of the words in brackets?

3. How does the writer let you know what the characters are doing (the action)?

4. How can you tell what the characters are like? Compare the characters of Suhail and Amy in the first play.

5. Try writing your own play based on a well known story.

Also available

by

Ian MacDonald

Published by

Educational Printing Services Limited

Mrs Wrelton's Dinosaur

ISBN 1-904374-48-4

Jeffa's Journey

ISBN 1-904374-91-3

The Snowspike

ISBN 1-904904-21-1

Please see our website www.eprint.co.uk for our
full range of publications